GRACE UNDER PRESSURE

GRACE UNDER PRESSURE

Inspirational Poetry of Comfort

Vernna L. Anderson Jr.

3274 12th Avenue N
Anoka, MN 55303

Order this book online at www.trafford.com
or email orders@trafford.com

Most Trafford titles are also available at major online book retailers.

Printed in the United States of America.

ISBN: 978-1-4269-5920-2 (sc)

Trafford rev. 03/07/2011

 www.trafford.com

North America & international
toll-free: 1 888 232 4444 (USA & Canada)
phone: 250 383 6864 ♦ fax: 812 355 4082

TABLE OF CONTENTS

Dedicated to my first mentors: Mr. Vernna L. Anderson Sr. and Mrs. Juanita S. Anderson, my father and mother.

GRACE UNDER PRESSURE

2 Corinthians 4:8-19

Matthew 6:19-21	Now this little treasure of mine
	Will only get richer over the test of time
Mark 10:21	Through sharing it with all my friends,
	Those unknown and those I have yet to see again;
Hebrews 4:14-16	I pray that these words become your own,
	Letting the Spirit show by grace that your suffering is not alone;
2 Timothy 3:14-17	These words were written from Scriptures and my heart
I Corinthians 10:13	To show that the whole world suffers in all its parts,
	But during each trial there is always a way out,
James 1:12	We must only endure; being proved without doubt;
James 1:13-16	For God Himself does not tempt any man—
James 1:17-18	Giving every good and perfect gift as only He can,
I Peter 4:13-19	Therefore suffer as a Christian, maintaining grace under pressure,
2 Corinthians 4:7-15	So your grace may abound to the glory of God's treasure.

POETRY WITH BIBLE SCRIPTURES OF COMFORT
WRITTEN AND COMPOSED BY VERNNA L. ANDERSON JR.
CHURCH OF CHRIST

A BIRTHDAY MEDITATION

BONNIE J BRANDT
PSALM 119: 9-16

Now that you're grown
You are now on your own;
Now your own lady,
No longer mommy's little baby;
Not daddy's little girl,
But a godly woman in this world;
The choice to choose as you please
And fulfill your own needs;
To do what you want to—
Keeping God's word forever before you;
Remember you must have love above all else,
The power of love takes you beyond yourself.

AN APPLICATION TO BE A FRIEND

PROVERB 18:24	This comes from a friend-to-be
	Who wants to be closer than a brother;
	I just want to be myself...........friendly
PROVERB 27:10	And never forsake you or another;
JOHN 15:13	For the love of my friends
	I will lay down my life;
HEBREWS 2:14, 15	For I do not fear death as the end,
1 JOHN 5:11	But as eternal life in Jesus Christ;
PSALM 41: 9	I am familiar, of whom you can trust,
JOB 19:14, 19	And I will never hate, betray, or forget you,
DUETERONOMY 13:6-8	Nor will I tempt you to other gods – no not us,
JOB 2:11	But will mourn with you and comfort you too;
LUKE 11:5-8	As a friend you can always partake of what's mine
PROVERB 17:17	Because I; your friend, will love at all times.

YOUR BROTHER VERNNA

BENEDICTION OF A PREACHER

EUGENE ECHOLS SR.
PART 1

1 CORINTHIANS 1:30	Because of God
	You are in Christ Jesus,
	And God made Christ to be our wisdom;
	By Christ we are put right with God,
1 CORINTHIANS 6:9-11	Being able to enter God's kingdom
1 CORINTHIANS 6:14	God raised the Lord from death,
	And with his power will also raise us,
1 CORINTHIANS 1:9	We were called into the fellowship of Christ - -
	God is faithful, In him put your trust,
1 CORINTHIANS 13:6	Rejoice with love in the truth
1 CORINTHIANS 13:7	Love gives up never:
	Its faith, its hope, nor its patience
1 CORINTHIANS 13:8	Love never fails, it lasts forever.

BENEDICTION OF A PREACHER

EUGENE ECHOLS SR.
PART 2

1 CORINTHIANS 1:6	The testimony of Christ was confirmed in him.
1 CORINTHIANS 1:8	Christ will also confirm you to the end,
	That you may be blameless in the day
	Of our Lord Jesus Christ coming again.
1 CORINTHIANS 9:19	Though free from all men,
	He made himself a servant to all;
	That he might win the more,
1 CORINTHIANS 9:23	Doing this for the gospel's call;
1 CORINTHIANS 9:24	He ran in the race to win:
1 CORINTHIANS 9:25	To obtain an imperishable prize,
1 CORINTHIANS 9:27	Bringing his own body into subjection,
	Being sure he, himself, was not disqualified,
1 CORINTHIANS 15:57	But thanks be to God for the victory gained;
1 CORINTHIANS 15:58	Knowing that his labor was not in vain.

BENEDICTION OF A PREACHER

EUGENE ECHOLS SR.
PART 3

2 CORINTHIANS 1:3	Blessed be God and Father of Christ
2 CORINTHIANS 1:4	Who comforts us in all our tribulations;
2 CORINTHIANS 1:5	For as the sufferings of Christ abound in us
2 CORINTHIANS 1:7	So also you will partake of the consolation,
2 CORINTHIANS 1:12	Rejoice in the testimony of our conscience,
	For we have had our conversation in this life
	In simplicity and godly sincerity,
2 CORINTHIANS 2:17	We speak in the sight of God in Christ
2 CORINTHIANS 3:4	And we have such trust through Christ toward God,
2 CORINTHIANS 3:5	It is not that we are sufficient of ourselves
	God's ability to do anything on our own – – we can't,
2 CORINTHIANS 3:6	He made us able ministers of the New Testament;
	Not of the letter of the law, which kills,
	But of the Spirit which gives life still.

BENEDICTION OF A PREACHER

EUGENE ECHOLS SR.
PART 4

2 CORINTHIANS 4:13	We, having the same spirit of faith,
	According as it is written,
	"I also believed and therefore I spoke,"
2 CORINTHIANS 4:14	Knowing that He who raised up the Lord Jesus
	Will also raise us up with Christ,
	And will present us with you,
2 CORINTHIANS 5:5	Having given us the Spirit of Life;
2 CORINTHIANS 5:17	Therefore if anyone is in Christ
	He is a new creation,
2 CORINTHIANS	God having reconciled us to Himself through Christ,
	Has given us the ministry of reconciliation,
2 CORINTHIANS 11:31	Who is blessed forever, knows that I am not lying.

BLESSED ARE THE DEAD WHO
DIE IN THE LORD FROM NOW ON:

OUR BROTHER REGGIE FINCH
MAY GOD BE WITH HIM
REVELATION 14: 13
PART 1

The dying of one body

Means life of another,

When resurrected through Christ;

As Reggie our brother.

Wearing the armor of light;

Through the darkness it glistens,

Because Brother Reggie had faith,

As a true, devoted Christian.

He served the Lord each day

From dawn to dusk,

One of his finest examples

He left for us

As he followed in Christ's footsteps,

Leading no one astray

Devoted to his Lord and Savior

In every which way,

BLESSED ARE THE DEAD WHO
DIE IN THE LORD FROM NOW ON:

OUR BROTHER REGGIE FINCH
MAY GOD BE WITH HIM
REVELATION 14: 13
PART 2

With the Christian attitude
In his work, home, and speech,
He left a message for us all;
To obey God's Word and teach
He served and believed in the hope of his calling,
Hoping we all standfast with fear... not falling.
But our brother was prepared
To meet his savior,
Showing nothing but the best
Of Christian behavior.
We pray that we too...
May be so worthy...
As to sit on Jesus' right,
As our brother, Reggie
Is so deserving.
JAUARY 9, 1985

BLESSED ARE THE POOR IN SPIRIT
FOR THEIRS IS THE KINGDOM OF HEAVEN

MATTHEW 5: 3
PART 1

PSALM 27:1

LUKE 1:50

EPHESIANS 4:25

1 PETER 1:12 – 25

If I fail
Before I go
I have no fear
Because I know
I have tried
Both time and again
And have not lied
To women and men
In passing the word
To each and one
Like it was heard
The day it was done
Even if it means
Only on soul is won.

BLESSED ARE THE POOR IN SPIRIT
FOR THEIRS IS THE KINGDOM OF HEAVEN

MATTHEW 5: 3
PART 2

JUDE	As I traveled
	By and by
MATTHEW 5:16	No soul was shining
	I wondered why
	But then I knew
2 PETER 3:14-16	I must go to them
	And bring them closer
	To trust in Him
MATTEW 28:18	To learn the power
2 PETER 3:17, 18	And the glory is He
MATTHEW 11:28	And that He alone
	Sets men free
ROMANS 5:2	From death by sin
GENESIS 3	Through the fruit of that tree.

BLESSED ARE THE POOR IN SPIRIT
FOR THEIRS IS THE KINGDOM OF HEAVEN

MATTHEW 5: 3
PART 3

ROMANS 5:12	Sin is death
ROMANS 5:19-21	But there is eternal life,
	A spiritual wealth
	With our Lord, Jesus Christ
1 JOHN 4: 6	Through hearing His word
MATTHEW 22:29	Proclaimed in the Bible,
JOHN 12:48	For which all men
ROMANS 14:12	Have been made liable- -
ROMANS 10:9-13	To believe, repent, confess,
ACTS 2:38	And be baptized for
MATTHEW 28:19	The remission of sins
REVELATION 2:10	To be prepared for the end;
ACTS 24:15	Unto the resurrection
	Of the just and unjust of men.

BLESSED ARE THE POOR IN SPIRIT:
FOR THEIRS IS THE KINGDOM OF HEAVEN

MATTHEW 5: 3
PART 4

ACTS 2:39	For the promise is unto you
	And as many as the Lord calls;
JOHN 5:28,29	To those who have done good - -
	The resurrection of life to all,
	And they that have done evil - -
	The resurrection of damnation will befall;
2 TIMOTHY 3:16, 17	So remember Scripture is inspiration
GALATIONS 6:10	For benevolence, preaching, and edification
ROMANS 16:16	To the churches of Christ
ROMANS 12:4, 5	And its many congregations
JAMES 1:25	To continue as Jesus commands - -
MATTHEW 22:14	For many are called,
	But few are chosen
MATTHEW 25: 34	To sit upon His right hand.

BLESS OUR FATHERS

PSALM 128: 4
PART 1

PSALM 68:5

> What is a father?
> Is he the one with child,
> Who has no time to spend
> Not even a little while:

DUETERONOMY 6:5-7

> Or the one who loves the LORD
> With all his heart, soul, and might,
> And teaches God's word to his children

PROVERB 22:6

> To keep it always before their sight ?

PSALM 127:3

> Children are a heritage from God

PSALM 127: 5

> Even having many is not to be ashamed,

EPHESIANS 6:4

> But to bring them up in the training
> And admonition of the Lord,

ISAIAH 63:16

> Remember God is our Father;
> Our Redeemer from Everlasting is His name.

BLESS OUR FATHERS

PSALM 128: 4
PART 2

PSALM 103: 13	A father pities his children
PROVERB 23:13	But does not withhold correction,
PROVERB 19:18	And disciplines while there is hope
PROVERB 23:14	To deliver a soul from destruction:
PROVERB 13:24	He who spares the rod hates his child,
	But the love for him brings prompt discipline,
EPHESIANS 6:4	Not to provoke to anger;
HEBREWS 12:7, 9	For there is no son whom a father does not chasten
MATTHEW 15: 4	A father must have honor and respect
PROVERB 22:15	Using the rod to drive out foolishness
GENESIS 18:19	Commanding his household to keep God's Word,
	To do righteousness and justice;
JOSHUA 24:15	So you can choose whom to serve....
	But me and mine will serve the LORD.

BLESS OUR MOTHERS

LUKE 11: 27, 28
PART 1

MATTHEW 19:5	We left our homes,
	Our fathers and mothers,
	To become as one
	Joined to another.
GENESIS 3:16	Because of the pain
	Our mothers went through,
GENESIS 1:28	Fulfilling the divine word…
	This one mom; is for you.
1 TIMOTHY 2:15	The Scriptures teach that a woman
	Will be saved in childbearing,
	If abiding in faith, love, and holiness,
	With self control;
	Keeping to the word she has been hearing.
PROVERB 19:26	We will never cause you dishonor
	Or ever give a reason for shame,
	We will always honor you
EPHESIANS 6:2	And never despise your name.

BLESS OUR MOTHERS

LUKE 11:27,28
PART 2

1 TIMOTHY 4: 6	You have always instructed us
	To be good ministers of Jesus Christ,
	Nourished in the words of faith
	And of the good doctrine
	Which we are carefully following for life.
1 PETER 5:14	You have always shown your love
PSALM 113: 9	Like a joyful mother should,
ISAIAH 66;13	Providing comfort and teaching
DEUTERONOMY 11:19	As only a mother could.
PHILIPPIANS 1:3	I thank my God upon every remembrance of you
1 THESSALONIANS 2:17	Having been taken away from you
	For a short time in presence, but not in heart.
	Endeavoring more eagerly to see your face too;
1 THESSALONIANS 2:19	Hoping it will be in the presence of our Lord,
	At His coming - - we both being a part.

BRETHREN TOGETHER IN UNITY

PSALM 133: 1
PART 1

JOHN 15:14	A friend of Christ is a friend indeed
JOHN 14:15	And these are the types of friends we need:
1 CORINTHIANS 12:12	As the body is one and has many members,
1 CORINTHIANS 6:12	All the members of that one body,
COLOSSIANS 1:24	Being many, are of Christ's body; the church – –
ROMANS 12: 4	Your functions will be missed after 20 November;
	But whoever is joined to the Lord
	Is one spirit with Him,
1 CORINTHIANS 12:18	God has set each member in the body
	Just as He pleased
ROMANS 12:5	To function as members of one another individually,
1 CORINTHIANS 12:24,25	Composing the body so that there should be no schism;
JOHN 14: 16	The Father has already given us another Helper here,
JOHN 14: 17	That will abide with us forever; the Spirit of truth,
	But you know Him, for He dwells with us
	And is in you,
1 PETER 1: 17	So when you have sojourned from here,
	for us, do not fear.

BRETHREN TOGETHER IN UNITY
PSALM 133: 1
PART 2

1 THESSALONIANS 1: 2	We give thanks to God always for you,
1THESSALONIANS 1:3	Constantly mentioning you in our prayers,
	Your work of faith,
	Labor of love and patience of hope
	In our Lord Jesus, who's true;
1 THESSALONIANS 1: 4	Brethren beloved by God, He has chosen you,
1 THESSALONIANS 2: 1	For we know that your visit to us was not in vain,
1 THESSALONIANS 2: 7	Being gentle, as a nursing mother
	Caring for her own children - -
1 THESSALONIANS 2: 8	Becoming dear to you, you shared the gospel
	And your lives too;
1 THESSALONIANS 2: 10	We and God are witnesses of your behavior - -
	Do not worry,
	It was holy, just, and blameless
	Among the believers,
1 THESSALONIANS 2: 11	You charged every one of us as a father
	Does his own children
1 THESSALONIANS 2: 12	To walk worthy of God who calls us
	Into His kingdom and glory;
2 THESSALONIANS 3: 1	Finally, we pray that God's word has free course - -
	This we trust.
2 THESSALONIANS 3: 3	Cause the Lord is faithful, who will establish you
	And guard us.

COMFORT EACH OTHER

1 THESSALONIANS 5: 11, 14

PHILIPPIANS 2: 20	I care enough to offer you the very best
PHILIPPIANS 2: 5–11	Of the Lord Jesus Christ, whom God has blessed:
1 CORINTHIANS 12:13	By one Spirit we are baptized into one body – –
1 CORINTHIANS 12:24, 25	So we as members should have the same care
	for each other,
1 CORINTHIANS 12:26	And if one of our members, suffer so do we all,
MATTHEW 5:19	From the least to the greatest sister or brother;
2 CORINTHIANS 1:3	Our Father of mercies is the God of all comfort,
2 CORINTHIANS 1:4	Who comforts us in all our tribulation,
	So we may be able to comfort those
	Who are in any trouble
2 CORINTHIANS 5:7	With that which we receive from God – –
	consolation and salvation.
PHILIPPIANS 2:1	Therefore in Christ, is comfort, love, fellowship,
PHILIPPIANS 2:2	Being likeminded; having the same love, unity,
	And being of one mind,
PHILIPPIANS 2:3	In meekness esteeming others better than ourself – –
PHILIPPIANS 2:4	Looking out not only for our own interests,
	But of other sometimes.

FRIENDS

JOHN 15:14

MARK 10:15	Become a child of God
2 CHRONICLES 2:7	And become a friend for life,
JAMES 4:4	Or become a friend of the world
EPHESIANS 5:30	And not a member of Christ;
1 CORINTHIANS 10 2	Do not have fellowship with demons,
1 JOHN 1: 3	But fellowship with the Father with us;
JOHN 15:15	For Christ has many friends
ISAIAH 12:2	If God's salvation – – you trust;
ECCLESIASTES 9:12	For no one knows his time
2 CORINTHIANS 5:10	But if it starts with the house of God first,
	What if you have no obeyed the gospel of God then?
1 PETER 4:18	Now if the righteous one is scarcely saved here,
	Where will the ungodly and sinner appear?

HAPPY ANNIVERSARY: THE WOODS

THE FIRST OF MANY
CHERYL AND LARRY

EZEKIEL 34:26	I pray for showers of blessings
	To fall upon your heads;
3 JOHN 3	I pray that you have prospered in all things
	And be in the best health you ever had;
LUKE 11:2	I pray you let God's will be done – –
	Have you noticed the Kingdom of God has come?
EPHESIANS 4:32	As God forgives sins, you also forgive each other
LUKE 11:4	And God will deliver you from the evil one;
1 CORINTHIANS 10:13	No temptation has overtaken you
	Except that which is common to man.
	But God will not allow you to be tempted
	Beyond what you are able to stand;
MATTHEW 19:4, 5	From the beginning when God united husband and wife
MATTHEW 19: 6–9	He intended for anniversaries to be for life.

SEPTEMBER 22,1986

HAPPY BIRTHDAY MY BROTHER

SEPTEMBER 24, 1986

PSALM 127:2	If you want another birthday, treat this year right,
	Don't go out and party - - go to sleep at night;
LUKE 8:14	Don't get caught up in the cares of this world - -
	Money, pleasures, material possessions,
	Or the arms of girls;
EPHESIANS 5:11	Don't associate with those in sin
1 TIMOTHY 4:16	And you will be saved now … and then;
2 TIMOTHY 2:15	Don't forget about God and always think,
EPHESIANS 5:28	Be helpful to your wife - - do the dishes in the sink;
EPHESIANS 6:4	Don't provoke your children, but
	Raise them with a smile
HEBREWS 12 8	Or God will treat you like an illegitimate child;
1 PETER 4:16	Don't forget to be a Christian in the things you do
	So God will be pleased, and you will too;
1 CORINTHIANS 13:11	Therefore don't do the don'ts and be a man,
1 CORINTHIANS 14:20	A child can't understand, but a mature brother can.

HAPPY 24ᵀᴴ ANNIVERSARY FATHER

PROVERBS
PART 1

PROVERB 4:1	Hear, my father, the instruction of a father,
	And give attention to know understanding;
PROVERB 4:2	For I give you good doctrine:
	Do not forsake the commanding,
PROVERB 4:3	When I was my father's son,
	He also taught me this to give:
	Let your heart retain my words;
	Keep my commands, and live,
PROVERB 12:4	You have found an excellent wife – –
PROVERB 18:22	A good thing you have done,
PROVERB 29:19	But no one abides by mere words;
	For though you understand – – respond,
PROVERB 3:7	In your own eyes do not be wise,
PROVERB 13:10	But with wisdom, be well- advised.

HAPPY 24ᵀᴴ ANNIVERSARY FATHER

PROVERBS
PART 2

PROVERB 10: 1	A wise son makes a glad father,
PROVERB 5: 1	So listen to my understanding;
PROVERB 14: 1	A good woman is like wisdom
PROVERB 4: 7	And this is the principle thing;
PROVERB 4: 6	Do not forsake her, but love her,
PROVERB 4: 13	Keep her, for she is your life,
PROVERB 4: 8	Exalt her, she brings honor with your embrace – –
PROVERB 5: 18	Rejoice with your wife;
PROVERB 3: 15	She is more precious then rubies,
PROVERB 3: 14	And her gain than fine gold,
PROVERB 3: 18	With the woman of whom you took hold,
PROVERB 5: 19	Let her breasts satisfy you at all times;
	And always be enraptured with her love.

AUGUST 26, 1986

25

HAPPY 24TH ANNIVERSARY MOTHER

SONG OF SOLOMON
PART 1

CANTICLES 1:1	Listen, my mother, to these words
	Of a woman who is in love;
CANTICLES 1:2	The husband's love is better than wine
CANTICLES 8:7	Which no wealth can take the place of,
CANTICLES 1:2	Let him kiss you with his kisses
CANTICLES 2:2	Because he rightly loves you,
CANTICLES 1:5	Your are dark, but lovely,
CANTICLES 5:1	His sister, but wife too,
CANTICLES 8:4	You have stirred up love;
CANTICLES 5:9	Choosing your beloved above another,
CANTICLES 8:4	Because it pleases you;
CANTICLES 8:1	His being a husband and a brother,
CANTICLES 3:4	Always seek the one you love
CANTICLES 5:2	And always welcome your beloved dove.

HAPPY 24TH ANNIVERSARY MOTHER

SONG OF SOLOMON
PART 2

CANTICLES 2:16	Your beloved is yours,
	And you are his,
CANTICLES 4:9	You have ravished his heart – –
CANTICLES 4:10	O how fair your love is;
CANTICLES 7:6	How fair and how pleasant you are,
	O love, with your delights.
CANTICLES 6:13	Remember to always return to your love
	That he may look upon your sight – –
CANTICLES 8:10	Peace you have found in his eyes,
CANTICLES 5:16	As he Is altogether lovely and a friend,
CANTICLES 2:12	The time of singing has come,
CANTICLES 6:10	From the morning to the end,
CANTICLES 7:8	Now let your breasts be like clusters of the vine,
CANTICLES 7:9	And the roof of your mouth like the best wine.

AUGUST 26, 1986

LOVE IS AS STRONG AS DEATH.

SONG OF SOLOMON 8:6
PART 1

ROMANS 5:14	Death has power from Adam to Moses,
	Even over those who had not sinned,
NUMBERS 35:30	But for those who kill another
HEBREWS 3:18	God will not let them enter in;
DEUTERONOMY 16:18	For just cause God allows judges
DEUTERONOMY 17:11	To pronounce sentence upon all men,
	For a person shall be judged
DEUTERONOMY 24:16	According to his own sin:
JOSHUA 1:18	Only be strong
	And of good courage,
DEUTERONOMY 16:20	And follow what is just
HEBREWS 9:15	In order to live and receive
	The promise of the eternal inheritance:
	This do as you must.

LOVE IS AS STRONG AS DEATH

SONG of SOLOMON 8:6
PART 2

ECCLESIASTES 5:7	But fear the Lord God
PSALM 48:13	And tell every following generation;
PSALM 48:24	He is our God forever and ever;
PSALM 68:20	He is the God of salvation:
JOHN 5:24	To him who hears Christ's Word
	And believes in his Father's name
	Shall pass from death into life
	And not be ashamed;
JOHN 5:25	For the hour is coming
	And now is,
	When the dead will hear
	The voice of the Son of God
	And those who hear
	Will live.

LOVE IS AS STRONG AS DEATH

SONG of SOLOMON 8:6
PART 3

ROMANS 6:3	As many of us as
	Were baptized into Christ
	Were baptized into his death
ROMANS 6:5	For the resurrection of life;
ROMANS 6:4	Therefore we were buried
	With Jesus through baptism
	And raised from the dead,
EPHESIANS 4:23	To be renewed in the spirit
	In which he has,
1 CORINTHIANS 15:57	But thanks be to God
	For the victory which is won;
JOHN 3:16	For God so loved the world
	That he gave his only begotten Son;
HEBREWS 10:17	Taking the sins away from everyone.

LOVE IS AS STRONG AS DEATH

SONG of SOLOMON 8:6
PART 4

ECCLESIASTES 3:2   There is a time to be born,
                    And a time to die;
ECCLESIASTES 3:4   A time to cry and mourn
                    Without asking why,
ROMANS 14:7   For we are the Lord's
                    Whether we live or die;
ECCLESIASTES 7:1   As the day of death is better
                    Than the day of our birth;
HEBREWS 2:10   For Christ is the author
                    Of salvation come to earth,
HEBREWS 9:27   And as it is appointed
                    Death and judgment to keep,
ROMANS 8:38   I am persuaded to die in the Lord;
MATTHEW 7:8   The love of God is what I seek.

LOVE IS AS STRONG AS DEATH

SONG of SOLOMON 8:6
PART 5

MARK 1:15	The time is fulfilled,
	The kingdom of God is at hand
MATTHEW 22:37	For those who love the Lord
	With all their heart, soul, and mind;
2 THESSALONIANS 2:16	For God's love has given us
	Good hope by grace,
REVALATION 24:4	And will wipe away the tears
	From everyone's face;
PHILIPPIANS 1:21	For me to live in Christ
	And to die is gain;
REVELATION 21:4	There shall be no more death.
	Nor sorrow, crying, or pain.
REVELATION 21:1	For the former things shall pass away
	Dawning toward the new day.
JOHN 14:6	With the love of the truth
	Jesus draws us to Himself,
1 JOHN 4:8	For God is love;
SONG OF SOLOMON 8:6	Love is as strong as death.

MAINTAINING PURITY IN THE FAITH

ROMANS 14:12–23
PART 1

ROMANS 14:12	Each of us shall give account of himself to God
ROMANS 14:13	So let us not judge one another anymore,
	But judge this rather, not to put a stumbling block
	Or cause to fall in our brother's way as before;
ROMANS 14:14	I know and am convinced by the Lord Jesus
	That there is nothing unclean of itself;
	But to him who considers anything to be unclean,
	To him it is unclean regardless of everything else;
ROMANS 14:15	Yet if your brother is grieved because of your food
	You are no longer walking in love – –
	Do not destroy him with your food for whom Christ died,
ROMANS 14:16	Therefore do not let your good be evilly spoken of;
ROMANS 14:17	For the kingdom of God is not food and drink,
	But righteousness and peace and joy in the Holy Spirit;

MAINTAINING PURITY IN THE FAITH

ROMANS 14:12–23
PART 2

ROMANS 14:18	For he who serves Christ in these things
	Is acceptable to God and approved by men by doing it;
ROMANS 14:19	So let us pursue the things which make for peace
	And the things by which one may edify another;
ROMANS 14:20	All things indeed are pure, but it is evil
	For the man who eats with offense to his brother;
	Do not destroy the work of God for the sake of food.
ROMANS 14:21	It is good neither to eat meat or drink wine
	Nor do anything by which your brother stumbles.
	Or is offended or is made weak at any time;
ROMANS 14:22	Happy is he who does not condemn himself
	In what he approved from his faith within;
ROMANS 14:23	But he who doubts is condemned if he partakes,
	For whatever is not from faith is sin.

OLD THINGS HAVE PASSED AWAY

REVELATION 21:4
PART 1

One minute in time
Is but a passing factor;
We cherish the memory:
It leaves nothing else after.
So we appoint things
And match them with times,
To help remind us all
To keep them on our minds.
The things not recalled
That we tend to forget;
We remember the things,
We just forget the time for it.
The things which were good
Kept happening as they should,
These times were extended
For as long as they could.

OLD THINGS HAVE PASSED AWAY

REVELATION 21:4
PART 2

The bad things in life
Always made us sad,
These are the times
We forget we had.
The things that we do:
These times are kept constant,
The things that we did
Were gone in an instant;
So remember the good times
Are the ones that last,
The bad memories
Are left in the past.

ONLY THE LOST

PART 1

MATTHEW 18:11	Only the lost
	Can complain,
LUKE 19:9-10	Especially if they
	Choose not the way
	To be ordained
	As a disciple
	Of Christ,
MATTHEW 28:19-20	And follow his word,
	Until one day
	The world has heard,
	Or until
	You yourself take part;
MATTHEW 10:32	And believe, repent, confess,
HEBREWS 11:6	And become baptized
ACTS 2:38	For the remission of sins,
	Before the end.

ONLY THE LOST

PART 2

EPHESIANS 3:4	You must read and understand
	The mystery of Christ;
EPHESIANS 5:13	How he died for all mankind,
	Being made manifest by the light.
HEBREWS 8:13	Making the first testament old
ROMANS 15:4	Which was written for our learning;
HEBREWS 8:6–12	Being the mediator of a better one,
	For which, we have all been yearning.
ROMANS 3:23	For all have sinned,
	And fell short of God's glory,
ROMANS 13:11	Now it's time to awake….
	There is no need to worry.
ROMANS 13:11	Now our salvation
	Is nearer than when we believed;
EPHESIANS 5:6	Be conscious of vain words,
	And be not deceived.

ONLY THE LOST

PART 3

ROMANS 13:12	The night is far spent,
	The day is at hand,
MATTHEW 15:3,9	Repent from vain worship;
	The commandments and traditions of men.
ROMANS 13:12	Cast off the darkness,
	And put on the armor of light;
ROMANS 13:13–14	Walk honestly as in the day,
	But put on the Lord Jesus Christ.
JOHN 5:39	Search the Scriptures;
	For in them
	You think you have eternal life,
	And they are they
	Which testify of Christ.
JOHN 8:31	If you continue in Christ's word,
	You are His disciples indeed,
1 TIMOTHY 4:16	And you shall save both; yourself,
	And them that hear thee.

ONLY THE LOST

PART 4

EPHESIANS 4:1	I therefore beg you;
	Come one, come all,
	Walk worthy of the vocation
	Wherewith you are called:
MATTHEW 7:7	To seek,
	And to find,
EPHESIANS 4:23	And to be renewed
	In the spirit of your mind.
COLOSSIANS 1:26	The mystery which has been hid,
	From ages and generations
	Is the riches of the glory,
COLOSSIANS 1:27	Which is Christ in you;
	The hope of the glory,
COLOSSIANS 1:28	Of whom we preach,
	Warning and teaching every man
	In all wisdom
COLOSSIANS 2:6	To receive Christ Jesus the Lord;
	And walk in him,
COLOSSIANS 2:7	Rooted and built up in Christ, the Living;
	And be established in the faith,
	As you have been taught;
	Abounding therein with thanksgiving.

OUR SAVIOR

ISAIAH 53
PART 1

ISAIAH 53:1	Who has believed our report?
	And to whom has God's arm been revealed?
ISAIAH 53:2	He has no form or comeliness
	Nor any beauty to appeal;
ISAIAH 53:3	He is despised and rejected by men,
ISAIAH 53:4	Surely He has borne our sorrows and griefs;
ISAIAH 53:5	He was wounded and bruised for our iniquities,
	Because He received the chastisement for our peace;
	Being healed by His wounds,
ISAIAH 53:6	God caused our sins to fall on Him;
ISAIAH 53:7	He was oppressed and He was afflicted,
	Yet was led as a lamb – – they slaughtered Him!
	And as a sheep before its shearers – –
	Still silent before them.

OUR SAVIOR

ISAIAH 53
PART 2

ISAIAH 53:8   He was taken from prison and from judgment,

And who will declare His generation?

For He was cut off from the living,

For the transgressions of God's people was He stricken;

ISAIAH 53:9   He made His grave with the wicked,

But with the rich when He died,

Because He had done no violence,

Nor was any deceit found justified;

ISAIAH 53:10   Yet it pleased God to bruise Him

When offering His soul for sin,

ISAIAH 53:11   Because His righteous servant

Will bear the world's sins

And justify many before the end;

ISAIAH 53:12   Therefore because of our transgressions,

We have forgiveness through His intercession.

SANCTIFICATION OF MARRIAGE: THE YOUNG'S

THE MARRIAGE OF SHERRY AND BARON
PART 1

GENESIS 1:27	In the beginning God made man,
GENESIS 2:18	But it is not good that man should be alone;
GENESIS 2:20	For there should be a helper for him – –
GENESIS 2:22	A woman a man can call his own;
GENESIS 2:24	Thus a man shall leave his father and mother
	And be joined to his wife,
	And they shall become one flesh
ROMANS 7:2	Bound together as one for life,
1 CORINTHIANS 7:33	But he who is married
	Cares about the things of the world – –
1 CORINTHIANS 7:34	How he may please his wife
COLOSSIANS 3:17	And the wife likewise, doing all in Christ,
MARK 10:9	Therefore what God has joined together,
	Let no man separate.

SANCTIFICATION OF MARRIAGE: THE YOUNG'S

THE MARRIAGE OF SHERRY AND BARON
PART 2

MALACHI 2:14	Because God is being a witness
	Between you and the wife of your youth,
1 JOHN 3:8	Let us not love in word or in tongue,
	But in deed and in truth;
EPHESIANS 5:22	Wives, submit to your own husbands
EPHESIANS 5:23	For the husband is head of the wife,
	As also Christ is head of the church,
1 CORINTHIANS 11:3	And the head of every man is Christ;
1 PETER 3:7	Likewise you husbands,
	Live with them with understanding;
	Giving honor to the wife
	As to the weaker body,
	And as being heirs together of the grace of life,
	That your prayers may not be hindered.

SHARE A CARE

PHILIPPIANS 4:10

To care is to show emotions:
Feelings of understanding, sensitivity, and caring;
To become a part of the other person,
After all you are partaking in sharing;
Giving a portion of what you have – –
A part of a big and wonderful heart;
You don't need words, knowledge, or experience,
Just your being there is a start;
The least you can do is be present,
Let them feel your warmth there;
Lend yourself to reach out and touch,
If you care, try, no matter what or where;
Who knows, you may think it's not too much
When you need someone to share a care and touch.

SHERRY AND HER WEDDING DAY

PART 1

PROVERB 10:22	Baron has found Sherry,
	And finding a good thing,
	He obtains favor from God – –
PROVERB 31:10	She is worth more then precious gain;
PROVERB 31:11	Baron's heart safely trusts her;
	She does him good all the days of her life,
EPHESIANS 5:25	Just as Christ loved the church,
	Baron also loves his wife;
PROVERB 31:15	She provides food for her household,
PROVERB 31:17	And strengthens her arms,
PROVERB 31:25	Strength and honor are her clothing;
	She shall rejoice in time to come,
PROVERB 31:28	Her children rise up and call her blessed;
	Her husband also, and he praises her.

SHERRY AND HER WEDDING DAY

PART 2

1 CORINTHIANS 13:4	Love is patient and kind;
	Love is not jealous or parades itself,
1 CORINTHIANS 13:5	Not puffed up, ill-mannered or selfish,
	Not provoked or thinks any evil above all else;
1 CORINTHIANS 13:6	Love does not rejoice in sin,
	But rejoices in what is true;
COLOSSIANS 3:13	Bearing with and forgiving one another,
	Even as Christ forgave you, so you also must do;
1 CORINTHIANS 13:7	Love bears and believes all things,
1 CORINTHIANS 13:8	Love hopes and endures all things forever;
HEBREWS 13:4	Marriage is honorable among all,
HEBREWS 13:5	Christ will leave you and forsake you never;
EPHESIANS 5:28	So Baron should love Sherry as his own body;
EPHESIANS 5:29	To nourish and cherish her,
	Like Christ does the church.

SUFFER AS A CHRISTIAN

1 PETER 4:12-19
PART 1

ROMANS 8:12-17	You are a Christian now
1 JOHN 4:17-19	So have no fear,
2 THESSALONIANS 2:16,17	Whatever you do
	Just keep Christ near,
	In word or deed
	Keep to the truth,
JOHN 14:26	Remember the things
	Taught from your youth,
1 TIMOTHY 6:11-16	Maintain the practice
	Of what you know is right,
2 CORINTHIANS 13:5,6	Tested and proven by the Spirit
	With all your might,
ROMANS 8:11	Because the Spirit is within
	Keeping you from sin.

SUFFER AS A CHRISTIAN

1 PETER 4:12-19
PART 2

1 CORINTHIANS 16:13	Stand fast in the faith
EPHESIANS 6:15	And the gospel of peace,
	Praying always in the Spirit
EPHESIANS 6:18	With all perseverance - - never cease,
TITUS 3:4-8	You are reborn through Christ
JOHN 3:3, 5	Having a spiritual birthday,
JOHN 14:16-18	Given the Comforter by God
	To always stay,
1 PETER 3:21	Having been saved by baptism
1 PETER 1:3-5	Through the resurrection of Christ,
JOHN 3:15-17	Because you believe…..
	You will have everlasting life;
MATTHEW 10:22	Being saved, enduring to the end,
JAMES 4:4-6	Staying pure from worldly friends.

SUFFER AS A CHRISTIAN

1 PETER 4:12–19
PART 3

2 TIMOTHY 2:10	Endure all things
	To be a chosen one,
ROMANS 5:17	Because the gift of Life
	Comes through the One;
GALATIANS 6:6–10	Do not be deceived
2 THESSALONIANS 2:9–12	By Satan's evil inventions,
	Receive the love of the truth
	And withstand Satan's intentions;
ACTS 8:22	Repent of wickedness
	And pray God to be forgiven,
PHILIPPIANS 4:3	To keep your name written
	In the Book of the Living;
MATTHEW 26:41	The flesh is weak,
	But the spirit indeed is willing.

SUFFER AS A CHRISTIAN

1 PETER 4:12-19
PART 4

ACTS 5:29	We ought to obey God
	Rather than man,
ROMANS 6:15-23	Becoming slaves of God
	Is the proper stand
1 CORINTHIANS 11:1	As imitators of Christ
EPPHESIANS 5:1	Being God's children,
MATTHEW 12:50	Doing the Father's will
MATTHEW 23:8	As sisters and brethren,
1 JOHN 2:15-17	Keeping from loving things in the world
	Keeping God's love in us,
	For all that is in the world
	Is passing away, including the lust…..
	Of the flesh, eyes, and pride of life – –
2 CORINTHIANS 2:10,11	These are not of God, but Satan's device.

SUFFER AS A CHRISTIAN

1 PETER 4:12-19
PART 5

GALATIANS 5:16	Walk in the Spirit
	To not fulfill the lust of the flesh,
1 THESSALONIANS 5:21,22	Abstain from every form of evil
	Put all things to the test,
	Hold fast what is good
1 PETER 1:22-25	Through God's word which lives forever;
	By which the gospel was preached to you
JOHN 10:35	And the Scripture cannot be broken ever,
2 PETER 1:1-4	Giving us all things pertaining
	To life and godliness:
GALATIANS 6:22,23	Adding love, joy, peace, longsuffering,
	Kindness, goodness, faithfulness,
	Gentleness, and self-control,
2 PETER 1:5-11	To make our calling and election sure, as told.

SUFFER AS A CHRISTIAN

1 PETER 4:12-19
PART 6

ROMANS 14:12   We are each responsible to God
       To give account of himself;

ROMANS 13:8-10   You shall love your neighbor
       Even as you love yourself,

MATTHEW 12:36, 37   And in the day of judgment:
       For every word you may have said,

2 CORINTHIANS 5:9-11   For every thing you have done
       Whether good for bad,

1 CORINTHIANS 3:20   Including every single thought
MATTHEW 5:28   And intent of the heart,
2 CORINTHIANS 9:6-8   Every reason for giving
       Cheerfully sharing a part,

JAMES 4:17   Therefore, to him who knows to do good within
       And does not do it, to him it is sin.

SUFFER AS A CHRISTIAN

1 PETER 4:12–19
PART 7

2 TIMOTHY 2:7	Consider what I am saying
	And the Lord will give you understanding
	In all things pertaining to life
2 TIMOTHY 2:3	As a good soldier of Jesus Christ;
2 TIMOTHY 2:11	For if we died with Him,
	We shall also live with Him;
2 TIMOTHY 2:12	If we endure,
	We shall also reign with Him;
	If we deny Christ
	He also will deny us eternal life;
2 TIMOTHY 2:13	If we are faithless, Christ's remains,
	Denying Himself cannot be done,
ACTS 14:22	We must through many tribulations
	Enter into God's kingdom.

THE GREATEST LOVE OF ALL

JOHN 3:16
PART 1

JOHN 3:16	For God so loved the world
ROMANS 5:8	His son died for you and me,
GALATIANS 5:1	So stand fast in the liberty
	By which Christ has made us free;
ROMANS 8:32	He who did not spare His own Son,
	But delivered Him up for us all,
ROMANS 11:21	Nor did God spare the natural branches
ROMANS 11:19–23	Who did not believe they could fall:
ROMANS 1:5	By disobedience to the faith
	Among all nations for His name,
ROMANS 9:33	Only whoever believes on Christ
	Will not be put to shame;
ROMANS 5:5	Because God's love has been poured out
	In our hearts
	By the Holy Spirit who was given to us.

THE GREATEST LOVE OF ALL

JOHN 3:16
PART 2

JOHN 3:16	He gave His only begotten Son
ROMANS 3:25	To be a propitiation by His blood;
GALATIANS 1:4	Who gave Himself for our sins,
	According to the will of our God,
ROMANS 5:18	He came with the free gift of righteousness
	To all men resulting in justification of life,
ROMANS 5:21	So grace might reign through righteousness
	To eternal life through our Lord Jesus Christ;
ROMANS 13:14	By putting on the Lord Jesus Christ
ROMANS 6:3	Through baptism into His death,
ROMANS 6:4, 5	That just as Christ was raised from the dead,
ROMANS 9:23-26	We too shall know spiritual wealth;
ROMANS 6:6	Having our old man crucified with Him,
	That the body of sin might be done away with.

THE GREATEST LOVE OF ALL

JOHN 3:16
PART 3

JOHN 3:16	Whoever believes in Him should not perish;
ROMANS 10:9	Believe God has raised Christ from the dead,
GALATIANS 2:16	Because we are not justified by works,
	But by faith in Jesus Christ instead:
ROMANS 1:17	The just shall live by faith
ROMANS 2:29	With circumcision of the heart,
ROMANS 12:1	To present your bodies a living sacrifice,
	Holy, acceptable to God, is doing your part;
ROMANS 6:18	Becoming slaves of righteousness,
ROMANS 8:30	Predestined, called, justified, and also glorified;
ROMANS 5:6	For when we were still without strength,
	For the ungodly, Christ died;
ROMANS 6:23	For the wages of sin is death,
	But God's free gift is eternal life in Christ.

THE GREATEST LOVE OF ALL

JOHN 3:16
PART 4

JOHN 3:16	But have everlasting life
ROMANS 1:16	And not be ashamed of the gospel of Christ;
GALATIANS 2:20	Having been crucified with Him – –
	Live by faith in this life
ROMANS 16:19	So your obedience can be known to all,
ROMANS 6:11	That you are dead indeed to sin,
	But alive to God in Christ Jesus our Lord,
ROMANS 7:11	Not being deceived by sin again;
ROMANS 15:13	Now may the God of hope fill you
	With all joy and peace in believing,
ROMANS 16:25	Who is able to establish you
	According to the gospel and Christ's preaching,
ROMANS 4:13	Making you an heir of the promise
ROMANS14:17	In the Holy Spirit in God's kingdom.
	In Christ's name, Amen.

TRUE VALUE OF FRIENDSHIP

JOB 28:13

PHILIPPIANS 4:8	First we saw each other's virtues
PSALM 19:12	Then we saw each other's faults;
1 CORINTHIANS 13:12	Maybe in the future we will see each other
	As true friends as we ought;
GENESIS 11:7	Hopefully not to be misunderstood,
JOHN 8:43	But listening to every word;
PHILIPPIANS 2:15	By paying attention to our emotions
	Without harm to what's inferred;
ECCLESIASTES 3:7	Being able to say what we please
1 SAMUEL 16:7	Revealing our inter-most self;
EPHESIANS 4:15	Speaking the truth to each other
2 CORINTHIANS 6:11	Opening our hearts above all else;
MATTHEW 24:35	For we know Heaven and earth will pass away,
1 THESSALONIANS 5:17	But I pray our friendship last… even that day.